The Zioness' Den

The Royalty Edition

An advance My Time With the Most High Workbook

by

Tara La Sean

The Lord's Prayer

Our Father (Ahayah) which art in Heaven, Hallowed be thy name. Thy kingdom come, Thy will be done in earth, as it is in Heaven. Give us this day our daily bread. And forgive us our debts as we forgive our debtors. And lead us not into temptation, but deliver us from evil: For thine is the kingdom, and the power, and the glory, forever.

Ahayah Bahasham Yashaya Wa Rawach

(In the name of the Father, the Son and the Holy Spirit)

Amen

Shalom Family!

I am very excited to bring you Book One in the Zioness' Den series; The Royalty Edition! For those of you who are already familiar with the My Time With The Most High format, you will be able to jump right in to this advanced series. If this is your first book in the series, then *welcome!-* and prepare to enjoy fun and challenging puzzles, writing prompts and a variety of Bible based learning activities to help you stay in the Word and retain more of what you learn.

Though all of the workbooks Ahayah has me put together are special, the Zioness' Den holds a special place in my heart because it focuses on the women of the Bible and can help shape and guide my sisters of all ages to become the Daughters of Zion we were created to be.

This is especially important because in today's society, young women are taught that being disrespectful, unrighteous and self-indulgent is perfectly acceptable behavior. In fact, if you are a celebrity, rich (aspire to be rich) or a member of a "royal" family, such behaviors are expected, if not encouraged. We can draw from countless movies, TV shows, books, stories and reality shows featuring the lives of celebrities as examples of this corrupted ideal.

As Daughters of Zion, we are the real ladies of the Royal Court and as such, we are held to a higher standard of morals and ethics. In this workbook we will explore what it means to be a true *sarai* in the Nation of Israel. We will learn the stories of some amazing women who exemplified the attributes we should all aspire to; having wisdom and courage, being virtuous, righteous and obedient, having discernment, being generous, willing to serve selflessly and being uncompromising concerning Truth.

This book is advanced and targets grades 9-12 though activities can be modified. The activities rely on the KJV Bible, the KJV Apocrypha and the Book of Jasher (R.H. Charles translation). I hope you will enjoy the workbook and draw closer to The Most High!

Barak Atha,

Sis. Tara~

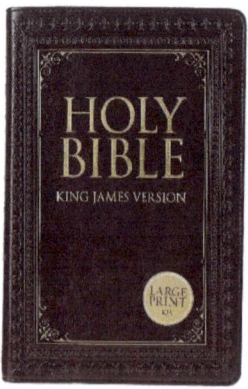 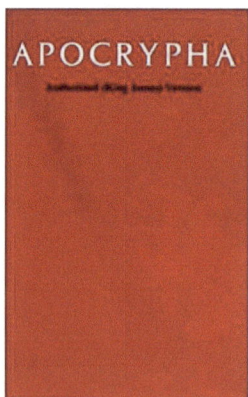 

*If you do not have these records by R.H. Charles, you can download them for free as a PDF to your personal device.

http://www.parsontom.com/books/Book%20of%20Jasher.pdf

IN ALL THY GETTING, GET UNDERSTANDING!

It is very important to understand the terms and concepts we will use in this workbook. Let's match the English term on the left to its Hebrew counterpart from the word bank. Then, look up the definition of the word and write it in the space.

> **CHOKMAH   AMETS   YIQHAH   CHAZAQ   YAHAB   CHAYIL   BIN   TSADDIQ   ABODAH**

1. Discernment _____:
_____
_____

2. Wisdom _____:
_____
_____

3. Serving _____:
_____
_____

4. Obedient _____:
_____
_____

5. Courage _____:
_____
_____

6. Resolute _____:
_____
_____

7. Virtue _____:
_____
_____

8. Righteous _____:
_____
_____

9. Generous _____:
_____
_____

The Princess who became Queen

Sarai: Princess of Obedience

In most cases when we think about Abraham's wife, we think about her being "Mother Sara;" blessed woman who gave birth in her old age. However, before she bore Isaac, she was known as Sarai, and was a very beautiful, wise, faithful and loving wife. In fact, she could be the basis for all the characteristics of a true, royal woman of The Most High. However, we will focus on her obedience in this section. Read the Book of Jasher chapter 15 to answer the following questions.

1. Where did Abram hide Sarai as they entered Egypt?

2. Why did Abram decide to hide her?

3. Before she was taken before the pharaoh, what did Sarai do?

4. What did Ahayah do to protect Sarai from the pharaoh?

5. Why did Abram and Sarai leave Canaan?

6. When the pharaoh first asked Sara who Abram was to her, what was her answer and why did she say it?

7. Upon hearing Sarai's initial answer concerning her relationship to Abram, what did the pharaoh do for him?

8. How does this story showcase Sarai's obedience?

9. Bonus Question: How does 1 Pet. 3:5-6 give more proof of Sarai's obedience?

All About Obedience

Find the words below which are all synonymous to obedience.

BIDDABLE
RESPECTFUL
ACQUIESCENT
DOCILE
LOYAL
YIELDING

DEVOTED
SUBSERVIENT
AMENABLE
DOCIOUS
OBLIGING

FAITHFUL
WILLING
COMPLIANT
HONORING
PLIANT

Build your vocabulary! Pick THREE words you do not know and write the definitions below.
_____
_____

Matched With Obedience

The bible emphasizes the importance of obedience in every aspect of our lives. Review the following verses and match them to the appropriate category.

Obedience to Parents   Obedience to Ahayah   Obedience to our Husbands

1. Matt. 7:21 _____
2. 1 Cor. 11:3 _____
3. Col. 3:20 _____
4. 2 John 1:6 _____
5. John 14:15 _____
6. Eph. 6:1 _____
7. Prov. 30:17 _____
8. Jam. 4:7 _____
9. Eph 5:22 _____
10. Ecc. 12:13 _____
11. Acts 5:29 _____
12. Ex. 20:12 _____
13. 1 Pet. 3:1 _____
14. Tit. 2:4-5 _____
15. Matt. 15:4 _____

It's not about where you were forced to begin…

It's about where you allow your **COURAGE** to let you end!

RAHAB: A PORTRAIT OF COURAGE

Let's read Joshua chap. 2, the story of Rahab. This remarkable woman was a study in courage in many ways, proving that where you start your journey with Ahayah is not as important as where you end it. Use her tale to discuss the following points.

Give a brief overview of Rahab; how her story began, what she did to change herself, protect the Israelite spies and ultimately save the lives of her family. Include how she was rewarded.
_____
_____
_____
_____
_____
_____

Soldiers with swords were looking for the Israelite spies intent on murdering them. Consider the consequences to Rahab and her family if she had been caught. Discuss what you think might have happened and how those possibilities proved her bravery.
_____
_____
_____
_____
_____
_____
_____

Sometimes we desire to make changes in our lives but we fear the unknown or the potential outcomes of turning away from familiar things, even if they are bad for us. Discuss Rahab's decision to help the Israelites and how her willingness to change was courageous.
_____
_____
_____
_____
_____
_____

Tales from the Apocrypha

The Book of Susanna

Oh, Susanna! Righteous and Resolute!

Read the story of Susanna in the Apocrypha to answer the following questions.

1. **Susanna was from which tribe?**
   a. Manasseh
   b. Ephraim
   c. Judah
   d. Issachar

2. **What was the name of the young youth who spoke up for Susanna?**
   a. Jeremiah
   b. Daniel
   c. Isaiah
   d. Ezra

3. **What two types of trees did the elder claim they found Susanna and the young man?**
   a. Mastick and Holm
   b. Oak and Holm
   c. Mastic and Juniper
   d. Fir and Pine

4. **Susanna was described as being which of the following?**
   a. Beautiful/ smart
   b. Very fair/ feared the Lord
   c. Pretty/ Righteous
   d. Cute/ Wise

5. **Why was Susanna alone when the elders came to her?**
   a. Her maids went to fix her lunch
   b. Her maids went to get her oils and bath balls
   c. Her maids were paid to leave by the elders
   d. The maids were meeting their young men

6. **Susanna was the daughter of _____ and wife of _____.**

7. **What reasoning did Susanna use when deciding whether or not she would do what the elders asked?**
   _____
   _____
   _____
   _____

The Power of Determination!

While the story of Susanna is certainly a wonderful example of how an Israelite woman should stand firm in her faith and righteousness, there are other women who showed a great deal of determination in their belief in Ahayah as well. Let's read about a couple more extraordinary women!

"Mama" Macabee in 2 Macabees from the Apocrypha was an exceptional woman. Give a brief account of her story and explain why what she did was such a great example of determination. Also tell what her story teaches us today about unwavering faith and endurance.

_____
_____
_____
_____
_____
_____
_____
_____
_____
_____
_____
_____
_____

Judith from the Apocrypha. Read the book of Judith and give a brief overview of what was happening during her time. Give details about who she was and a few details about her character. Explain how what she did was an example of resolution and discernment.

_____
_____
_____
_____
_____
_____
_____
_____
_____
_____
_____
_____
_____

A man's gift maketh room for him, and bringeth him before great men.

Proverbs 18:16

JOANNA: A Truly Cheerful Giver!

Read the short passage about Joanna in Luke 8:3 which discuss how she ministered to Yashaya through her substance. This woman was a sterling example of how generous we should be towards each other, the less fortunate and to the ministers who do the work of Ahayah. Let's review the following scriptures and match them to one of the following categories. Be sure to explain why you chose that category. Remember, some passages may fit into more than one category!

GENEROSITY TO THE POOR   GENEROSITY TO EACH OTHER   GENEROSITY TO THE CHURCH

Ps. 41:1
_____
_____

1 Tim. 5:7
_____
_____

Lev. 27:30-32
_____
_____

Neh. 10:35
_____
_____

2 Cor. 9:7
_____
_____

Mark 12:42-44
_____
_____

Heb. 13:7
_____
_____

Phil 4:15-19
_____
_____

Gen. 28:20-22
_____
_____

Matt. 25:34-40
_____
_____

Generous, Ministering Women

Yashaya spoke several times throughout the Bible on the importance of being generous. Let's review the following women from the passages below and discuss how they were examples of Christ's message. Include who they were, what they did and why it was important. Advanced students should include at least **two** additional scriptures to support their answers.

Matt. 27: 55-56

_____
_____
_____
_____
_____

Acts 9:36-42

_____
_____
_____
_____
_____

Honorable Mention: Generous Woman from the Nations...

2 Kings 4:9-10

_____
_____
_____
_____
_____

Feminine Courage

Read the book of Numbers chapter 27: 1-11. Explain what the five daughters of Zelophehad did and why it was so important. Also explain why their actions were considered brave?

_____
_____
_____
_____
_____
_____
_____
_____
_____
_____

Exodus 1 tells us the story of Shiphrah and Puah, two Hebrew women who were asked to go against The Most High. Explain who these women were and what they did that was so courageous.

_____
_____
_____
_____
_____
_____
_____
_____
_____
_____
_____

Honorable Mentions...

While the Bible is full of Hebrew women who were brave and accomplished many wonderful things by the power of Ahayah, it is important to note some of the women from other nations whom He used to raise up, deliver or assist His people.

If you read Judges 4 you will learn about the role played by Jael, a woman from the nations. Discuss who she was and what she did for the Children of Israel. Be sure to include a brief history on what was happening that led to her heroism.

_____
_____
_____
_____
_____
_____

Ahayah sent Moses an amazing woman to be his wife. Though Zipporah was not born an Israelite, she exemplified many of the characteristics of a righteous Hebrew woman. Read Chapters 77 and 79 in the Book of Jasher to answer the following questions about this remarkable woman.

1. How did Zipporah support Moses when he was in ward, and for how long did she do it?
   _____
   _____
   _____
   _____

2. Ex. 4:24-26 discusses a brave act Zipporah did to save Moses and Gershom. Read Chapter 79 in Jasher to further understand the importance of her actions. Tell why you think this act makes her worthy of being an Honorable Mention among the courageous women of Israel?
   _____
   _____
   _____
   _____

3. Which four women do the scriptures compare Zipporah's righteousness to?
   _____
   _____

WHO AM I?

1. I am the daughter of a king and wife of a priest. When an evil woman put to death all those in the righteous royal family, I showed courage by kidnapping my nephew, son of the previous king, and hid him for six years. My story is told in II Kings. Who am I?

   _____
   _____

2. My husband and I are from the tribe of Dan and one day an angel of Ahayah appeared unto us and told us many wondrous things, including that I should bear a son though I had been barren. The Angel instructed us to raise the boy as a Nazarite. My husband was afraid for our lives when the angel left but I calmed him with words of truth and wisdom. Who am I?

   _____
   _____

3. I was married to the eldest son of a Hebrew man. When my husband died, I married his brother according to the custom. His brother dealt wickedly with me and I was left a widow with no children again after Ahayah struck him dead also. When their father refused to honor the agreement to have the youngest son marry me, I disguised myself as a harlot and seduced him. Who am I?

   _____
   _____

4. I am a prophetess. I married young but have been a widow for 84 years. I spent my years serving the Living God Ahayah through fasting and prayer. I gave thanks to the Lord and spake of him to all that looked for redemption in the temple in Jerusalem. Who am I?

   _____
   _____

5. I am a Benjaminite woman married to a Persian king. I was able to expose the wicked plot against my people by an evil Agagite. Who am I?

   _____
   _____

6. I am a young woman from Shunam who is noted for my beauty. I was a servant to a king in his old age and one of my duties was to lie next to him to keep him warm. Who am I?

   _____
   _____

7. I am a daughter of Levi who lived in Egypt. When a wicked ruler decreed that all Israelite sons be killed, I hid my youngest son for three months, then placed him in a basket and floated him down the river. Who am I?

   _____
   _____

WISDOM FROM ON HIGH

Before we delve into examples of women whose wisdom was legendary, let's first examine the Mother of all wisdom; the Ultimate Feminine Essence, the Rawach Qadash. Read the following passages to answer the questions and gain understanding how we know the Holy Spirit is female.

1. Read Wisdom of Solomon chapter 9. Where does the Rawach sit?
   _____
   _____
   _____
   _____

2. What is the first step towards wisdom? Read Prov. 9.
   _____
   _____
   _____
   _____

3. What does Luke chapter 7 say about wisdom?
   _____
   _____
   _____
   _____

4. The Book of James first tell us that if we lack wisdom we should ask _____. That same book later tells us the attributes of wisdom from above. What are they?
   _____
   _____
   _____
   _____

5. Prov. 19 gives us two tips on how to become wise. What are they?
   _____
   _____
   _____
   _____

6. There are several scriptures that tells us what the beginning of wisdom is. Besides the passage in Proverbs, find at least three more verses that tells us this.
   _____
   _____
   _____
   _____

7. Read Wisdom of Solomon ch. 6 and note each verse that refers to the Holy Spirit as a female.
   _____
   _____
   _____
   _____

Miriam: Big Sister, Leader and Prophetess

What do YOU think?

In some Hebrew circles it is believed that only the men of the Bible were leaders, teachers, judges or prophets of Israel. Sadly, what is often overlooked are the many women who served in these functions in appropriate and righteous ways. Let's start by examining Miriam and the wisdom of women in scripture. Read the following scriptures to answer the questions and tell how you think each passage relates to Miriam or shows the importance of wisdom.

1. Read Acts 2:17-18 and Joel 2:28 and tell what the scriptures say about women being prophets.
   _____
   _____
   _____

2. Read 1 Cor. 12:1-10 and explain what the scriptures say prophesy is.
   _____
   _____

3. Look up the Hebrew word and definition for prophecy and tell what part of speech it is and if it is a masculine or feminine word.
   _____
   _____
   _____

4. Read Acts 21:9 and tell what you think this story adds to our information about women prophets?
   _____
   _____
   _____

Character Traits of a Wise Woman

Write the letter of the correct match next to each problem.

1. _____ 1 Tim. 3:11 — a. Every wise woman buildeth her house: but the foolish plucketh it down with her hands.

2. _____ Titus 2:4 — b. Wisdom is glorious, and never fadeth away: yea, she is easily seen of them that love her, and found of such as seek her.

3. _____ Prov. 14:1 — c. Let the word of Christ dwell in you richly in all wisdom; teaching and admonishing one another...

4. _____ Wis. of Solomon 1:6 — d. Wives, submit yourselves unto your own husbands, as unto the Lord.

5. _____ Col. 3:16 — e. For wisdom is a loving spirit; and will not acquit a blasphemer of his words: for God is witness of his reins, and a true beh

6. _____ Prov. 31:26 — f. Even so must their wives be grave, not slanderers, sober, faithful in all things.

7. _____ Eph. 5:22 — g. Who is as the wise man? and who knoweth the interpretation of a thing? a man's wisdom maketh his face to shine,...

8. _____ Ecclesiastes 8:1 — h. That they may teach the young women to be sober, to love their husbands, to love their children,

9. _____ Wis. of Solomon 6:12 — i. She openeth her mouth with wisdom; and in her tongue is the law of kindness.

Deborah at the palm tree.

And More Wise Women...

Wisdom is such a key factor of being a true Daughter of Zion that we must delve into a few more stories about women who were sterling examples of this trait. Read about each of the following women and tell **who** they were, **where** they lived, **what** they did and **why** they are considered great examples of wise women.

Deborah Judges 4

Wise Woman of Tekoa 2 Sam. 14

Wise woman of Abel-beth-maachah

Foolishness and Folly Among Females...

Just as there are many wise women in scripture, there are also those who were prone to folly, vanity, corruption and downright foolishness. By learning the stories of a few silly women, we can learn what _**not**_ to do as princesses of Israel!

Read the story of the Ten Virgins in Matthew Chapter 25:1-13. Discuss what choices the foolish virgins made and the consequences of those actions. How does this relate to us today?

_____
_____
_____
_____
_____

Consider the tale of Sapphira in Acts 5:1-10. Explain what she did that was so unwise and what the penalty for her decision was. What can we learn from her?

_____
_____
_____
_____
_____
_____

When Brains met Beauty; A True Tale of Discernment

Abigail: One of Ahayah's Leading Ladies

Go back and refresh your memory on the definition of discernment, then read the story of Abigail in 1 Sam. 25. Answer the following questions.

1. Who was Abigail and what did she do that was so important?

   _____
   _____
   _____
   _____
   _____

2. Why is Abigail noted as a woman with discernment? Use specific examples and tie it to the definition.

   _____
   _____
   _____
   _____
   _____

3. Using the previous lessons on wisdom, how does discernment relate to wisdom? Be sure to give at least three scriptures to support your answer.

   _____
   _____
   _____
   _____
   _____

4. Besides wisdom, discernment relates to several other attributes of a proper Israelite woman. Choose two more characteristics and show the connection to discernment. Again, be sure to give at least two scriptures to support your answers.

   _____
   _____
   _____
   _____
   _____

Importance of Discernment

Use the words in the list below to complete the sentence

> Prove rudiments acceptable, understanding philosophy prophets judgment Discerner piercing wholesome

1. Beloved, believe not every spirit, but try the spirits whether they are of God: because many false _____ are gone out into the world.
2. Judge not according to the appearance, but judge righteous _____
3. _____ all things; hold fast that which is good.
4. Give therefore thy servant an _____ heart to judge thy people, that I may discern between good and bad: for who is able to judge this thy so great a people?
5. And be not conformed to this world: but be ye transformed by the renewing of your mind, that ye may prove what [is] that good, and _____ and perfect, will of God.
6. If any man teach otherwise, and consent not to _____ words, [even] the words of our Lord Yashaya Ha Maschiac, and to the doctrine which is according to godliness;
7. Beware lest any man spoil you through _____ and vain deceit, after the tradition of men, after the _____ of the world, and not after Christ.
8. _____ For the word of God [is] quick, and powerful, and sharper than any twoedged sword, _____ even to the dividing asunder of soul and spirit, and of the joints and marrow, and [is] a _____ of the thoughts and intents of the heart.

Who can find a Virtuous Woman?
Isaac Did!

Focus on Virtue!

Mother Rebekah was truly a virtuous woman in every sense. In addition to the account given of her in Genesis 24, let's also read chapter 26 in Jasher to further understand how she was a model of virtue. Find a specific example from scripture of how Rebekah showed her virtue in each of the following areas.

1. Virtue in **Modesty**:
   _____
   _____
   _____
   _____

2. Virtue in **Faith:**
   _____
   _____
   _____
   _____

3. Virtue in **Obedience**:
   _____
   _____
   _____
   _____

4. Virtue in **Discernment:**
   _____
   _____
   _____
   _____

5. Virtue in **Wisdom**:
   _____
   _____
   _____

6. Virtue in **Hospitality**:
   _____
   _____
   _____
   _____

The Many Female Faces of Virtue
Complete the crossword below using the KJV Bible.

Across
3. Early female believer from the Church at Colossae, referred to by Paul as 'our sister' and 'dearly beloved.'
5. I am a midwife who refused to follow the wicked instruction of the pharaoh.
6. Originally from Thyatira, a dealer in purple and early member of the Church in Philippi.
8. The second beautiful daughter of Job.
9. I am the grandmother of Timothy and my daughter Eunice and I were believers.

Down
1. My husband and I are tent makers and worked in ministry with the Apostle Paul.
2. I am the eldest daughter of Job.
4. I am a worker in the Cenchrean Church and Paul refers to me as 'our sister.'
5. I am a faithful follower of Yashaya and like Joanna and other women, supported Him with my finances.
7. After my son died, his young widow stayed with me and accompanied me back to my hometown.

Royals Running Amok: The Cautionary tales of Vashti, Salome, Athaliah and Queen Jezebel

Being an evil or wicked woman is bad enough in itself. But imaging being that way with money, power and influence. Let's examine how these royal women abused their power to cause mischief and inflict suffering.

Salome and her Mean, Malicious Mama

Just as the righteous women took their cues from their mother, so did wicked women follow their evil predecessors. Let's read the story of "princess" Salome and her mother Herodias in Matt. 14:1-12 and Mark 6:14-29 to answer the following questions about this decidedly bad girl.

1. Why did Herodias despise John the Baptist? Give details about what she was doing and why it was sinful. Advanced learners should include Old Testament laws to illustrate your point.

   _____
   _____
   _____
   _____
   _____
   _____
   _____
   _____

2. How did Salome earn a reward from the king?

   _____
   _____
   _____
   _____
   _____
   _____

3. What did she ask for and why?

   _____
   _____
   _____
   _____
   _____
   _____
   _____

The Bold and the Beautiful; the Vain and the Vicious:
Vashti and Athaliah

Read the story of Queen Vashti in Esther chapter 1. First, describe what she did that caused the king to be offended. Then explain what the consequences of her actions were and why the king's counselors insisted the steps be taken against her. Be sure to explain what that punishment was and if you feel there was a scriptural basis for it and if it was fair.

_____
_____
_____
_____
_____
_____
_____
_____
_____
_____
_____

On the outset, we may believe that Athaliah's evil was based on her being a murderess. However, she was guilty of many other sins including usurping authority over men. Give the definition for the word **usurp** and discuss how her actions were in opposition of Gen. 3:16 and 1 Tim. 2:12.

_____
_____
_____
_____
_____
_____
_____
_____
_____
_____
_____

Wicked Beauty: The Story of Jezebel

Jezebel broke nearly every law The Most High ever gave and caused her weak-willed husband to do the same. Review the 10 Commandments listed in Ex. 20 and use the following passages to link her to these sins. Give the reason (s) why you feel she is guilty of breaking each law based on her actions in that scripture. Advanced students should be able to add at least two precepts to their answers.

1 Kings 19:1-2   1 Kings 21:5-25   2 Kings 9   1 Kings 16:31-33   1 Kings 18:4-19

1. _____

2. _____

3. _____

4. _____

5. _____

Shalom Family,

What an exciting journey we've had learning about our famous (and sometimes infamous) mothers and sisters. We have learned so much about the character traits of being a Daughter of Zion, or, as we saw in several examples, a righteous woman of any Nation! I don't know about you all, but I feel inspired to be better and do more to develop these traits.

I thank you all for joining me on this adventure into *The Zioness' Den* and I pray you have been edified and encouraged by reading the accounts of our kinswomen. For those of you who have completed other workbooks in the *My Time With The Most High* series, you were already familiar with the section titled the Zioness' Den, and after such positive response I decided to expand that section into its own mini-series. So stay tuned for *The Zioness' Den: The Fruit of the Spirit* edition!

This segment was also a lot of fun to create because it allowed me additional time to fellowship with many of the ahchwathyam from the Dallas body as they dressed up and posed for the pictures. I love and thank every one of you for your support! A special thanks to my "T-3 Twin" for agreeing to portray a bad girl so opposite from her true character. Thanks to the Ahchs who worked so hard to take the pictures and design the covers. And of course, I must give a special thanks to my local Bishop for supporting this work. His genuine support and encouragement have kept me motivated!

But the biggest THAWADAH of all goes to Abba Nawa, Ahayah Ashar Ahayah and His son Yashaya without Whom I could do nothing.

Barak Athan~

Sis Tara

ANSWERS

All About Obedience

Find the words below which are all synonymous to obedience.

K	U	F	B	R	Z	T	C	V	Y	K	I	D	Z	W	M	B	L	T
O	Q	S	R	K	B	Z	K	H	X	L	B	T	V	K	O	I	T	G
E	S	D	A	V	A	M	V	C	M	C	W	S	A	U	C	X	P	W	K
N	B	E	D	D	T	M	F	Z	I	V	E	L	V	X	B	A	T	D
K	B	T	D	A	N	S	E	X	L	O	S	F	U	S	F	I	N	X	O
H	B	O	U	Q	E	Z	T	N	Y	P	Q	Q	A	G	G	E	B	B	C
M	O	V	Y	E	C	E	R	N	A	A	J	P	P	I	I	U	W	U	I
E	T	E	O	N	S	E	L	A	A	B	Y	P	D	V	T	O	P	C	O
S	Y	D	T	Y	E	L	A	B	E	I	L	L	R	Y	L	H	I	X	U
E	R	G	M	I	I	Z	P	A	O	L	E	E	U	Z	L	F	F	S
Q	L	J	W	H	U	C	C	E	J	D	S	P	F	Q	H	E	C	U	N
P	K	X	P	E	Q	O	R	M	V	B	D	T	M	Y	T	O	Q	A	L
L	Z	H	C	C	D	A	R	U	X	C	I	T	O	W	J	D	A	S
K	A	C	Y	W	A	Y	Y	S	I	E	G	R	B	Z	C	T	L	V	H
W	Q	Y	C	I	M	Q	Q	P	K	P	I	B	W	I	T	L	I
F	W	K	O	L	H	F	W	S	R	L	O	Z	F	B	D	I	Q	J	K
K	D	Q	L	L	I	S	E	C	I	E	H	X	A	S	L	S	Q	I	O
P	M	F	X	I	Y	R	Z	A	D	Z	Q	O	B	L	I	G	I	N	G
W	O	O	G	N	N	I	D	L	E	I	Y	L	X	P	Q	P	J
Z	C	O	I	G	K	T	H	O	N	O	R	I	N	G	P	P	K	V	W

BIDDABLE   DEVOTED   FAITHFUL
RESPECTFUL   SUBSERVIENT   WILLING
ACQUIESCENT   AMENABLE   COMPLIANT
DOCILE   DOCIOUS   HONORING
LOYAL   OBLIGING   PLIANT
YIELDING

Character Traits of a Wise Woman

Write the letter of the correct match next to each problem.

Created on TheTeachersCorner.net Match-up Maker

1. __f__ 1 Tim. 3:11
2. __h__ Titus 2:4
3. __a__ Prov. 14:1
4. __e__ Wis. of Solomon 1:6
5. __c__ Col. 3:16
6. __i__ Prov. 31:26
7. __d__ Eph. 5:22
8. __g__ Ecclesiastes 8:1
9. __b__ Wis. of Solomon 6:12

a. Every wise woman buildeth her house: but the foolish plucketh it down with her hands.

b. Wisdom is glorious, and never fadeth away: yea, she is easily seen of them that love her, and found of such as seek her.

c. Let the word of Christ dwell in you richly in all wisdom; teaching and admonishing one another...

d. Wives, submit yourselves unto your own husbands, as unto the Lord.

e. For wisdom is a loving spirit; and will not acquit a blasphemer of his words: for God is witness of his reins, and a true beh

f. Even so must their wives be grave, not slanderers, sober, faithful in all things.

g. Who is as the wise man? and who knoweth the interpretation of a thing? a man's wisdom maketh his face to shine,...

h. That they may teach the young women to be sober, to love their husbands, to love their children,

i. She openeth her mouth with wisdom; and in her tongue is the law of kindness.

The Many Female Faces of Virtue

Complete the crossword below using the KJV Bible.

Across

3. Early female believer from the Church at Colossae, referred to by Paul as 'our sister' and 'dearly beloved.' (**claudia**)
5. I am a midwife who refused to follow the wicked instruction of the pharaoh. (**shiphrah**)
6. Originally from Thyatira, a dealer in purple and early member of the Church in Philippi. (**lydia**)
8. The second beautiful daughter of Job. (**keziah**)
9. I am the grandmother of Timothy and my daughter Eunice and I were believers. (**lois**)

Down

1. My husband and I are tent makers and worked in ministry with the Apostle Paul. (**priscilla**)
2. I am the eldest daughter of Job. (**jemima**)
4. I am a worker in the Cenchrean Church and Paul refers to me as 'our sister.' (**phoebe**)
5. I am a faithful follower of Yashaya and like Joanna and other women, supported Him with my finances. (**susanna**)
7. After my son died, his young widow stayed with me and accompanied me back to my hometown. (**naomi**)

www.ingramcontent.com/pod-product-compliance
Lightning Source LLC
Chambersburg PA
CBHW042027150426
43198CB00002B/89